NATURE FUN FACTS
MAZES

Tony J. Tallarico
and Tony Tallarico

DOVER PUBLICATIONS
GARDEN CITY, NEW YORK

Bibliographical Note

Nature Fun Facts Mazes, first published by Dover Publications in 2017, contains all thirty-five puzzles from the previously published *Nature Trivia Mazes* (2007) plus eleven new puzzles.

International Standard Book Number

ISBN-13: 978-0-486-81582-4
ISBN-10: 0-486-81582-X

Manufactured in the United States of America
81582002
www.doverpublications.com

You will learn some surprising facts about nature as you enjoy these 46 challenging mazes. In this exciting book, you'll find out how many colors make up a rainbow, how long a blue whale can go without eating, how many varieties of apples are grown in the world, which insects have the strongest legs, and much more. The end of each maze holds the answer to each piece of nature trivia. To make your journey even more fun, many of the mazes contain appealing illustrations that relate to the trivia, such as animals, fruits, insects, and trees, and you can color these in either before or after you solve the puzzles. Try your hardest, but if any of the mazes have you stumped, there is a Solutions section that starts on page 47.

The cheetah can reach a speed of 70 M.P.H., making it the fastest animal in the world. What is the second fastest animal, with a speed of up to 61 M.P.H.?

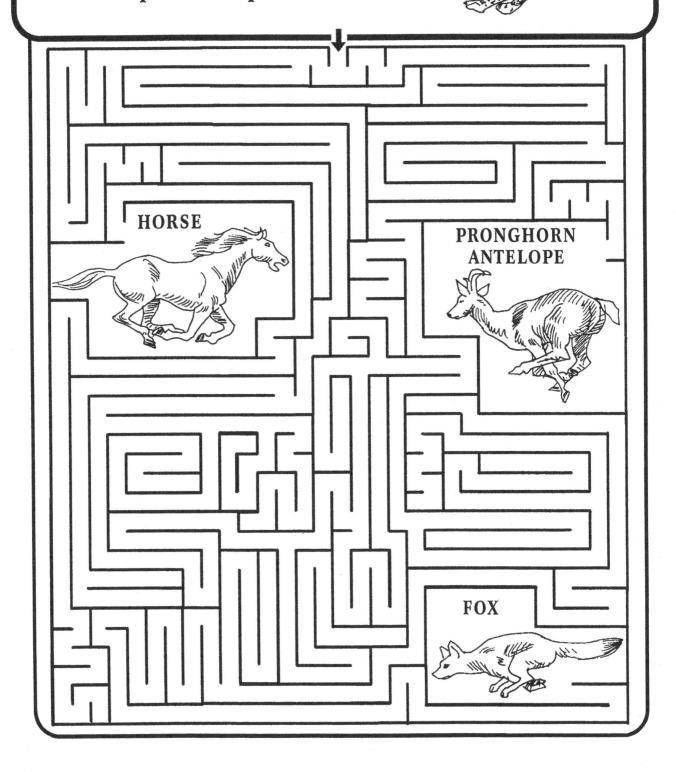

HORSE

PRONGHORN ANTELOPE

FOX

What color are flamingoes when they are born? (It's not pink!)

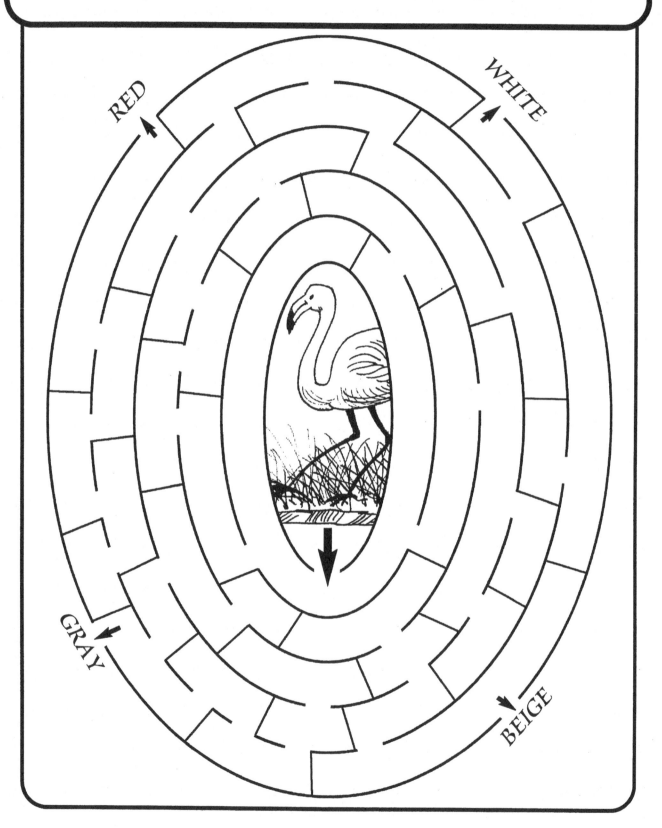

RED

WHITE

GRAY

BEIGE

Which of these dogs is known as the "barkless dog"?

TERRIER

KOMONDOR

BASENJI

CORGI

Americans eat more of these than any kind of fresh fruit, averaging over 25 pounds of them per person, per year!

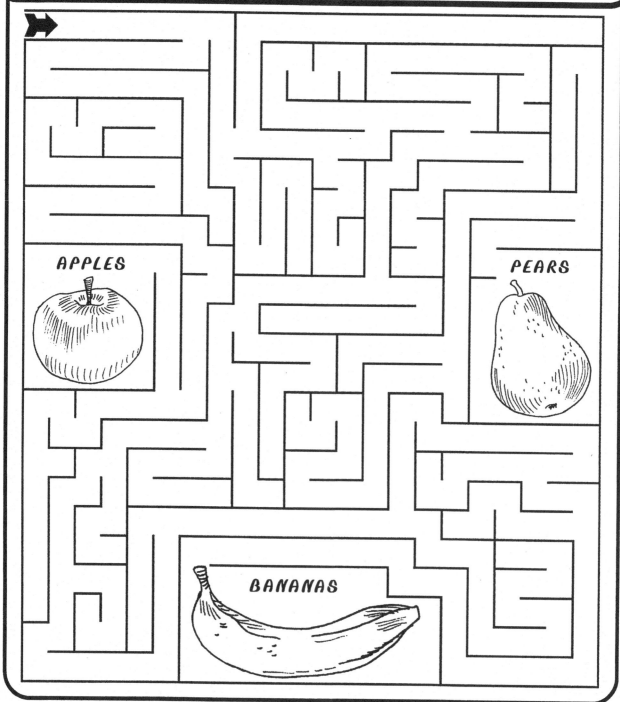

APPLES

PEARS

BANANAS

What family of animals does the koala belong to?

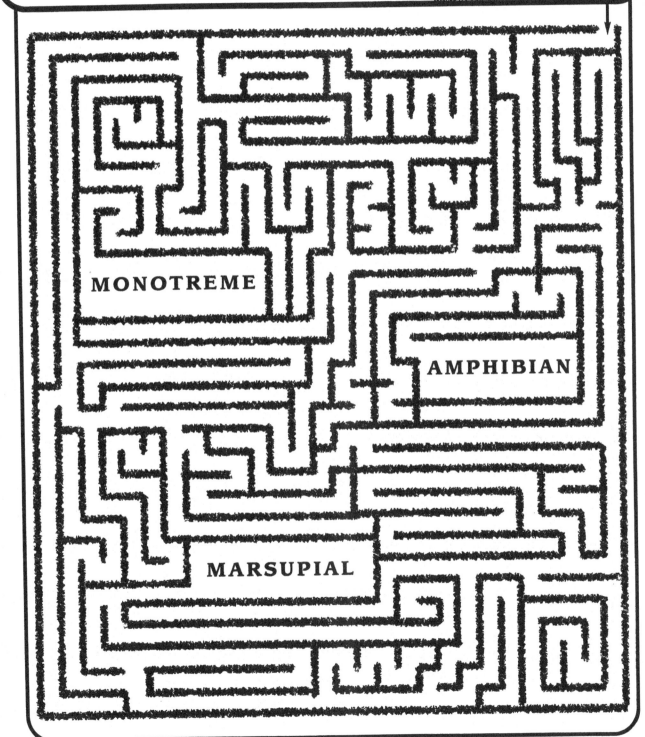

MONOTREME

AMPHIBIAN

MARSUPIAL

A PEANUT IS NOT A NUT!
WHAT IS IT?

A SEPAL

A GLUME

A LEGUME

6

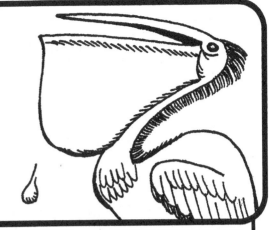

3 GALLONS

6 GALLONS

4 GALLONS

This is the largest of all rodents. A fully grown adult can weigh over 100 pounds!

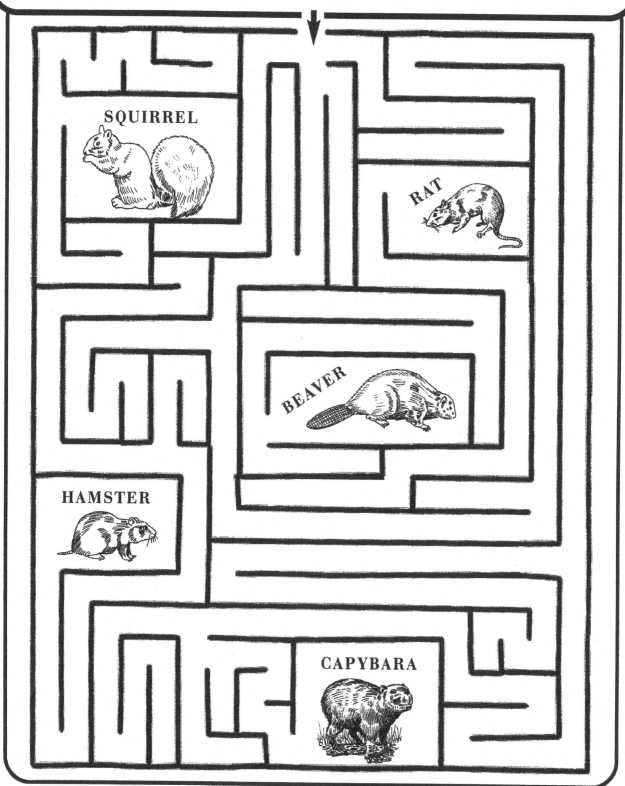

What is a group of leopards called?

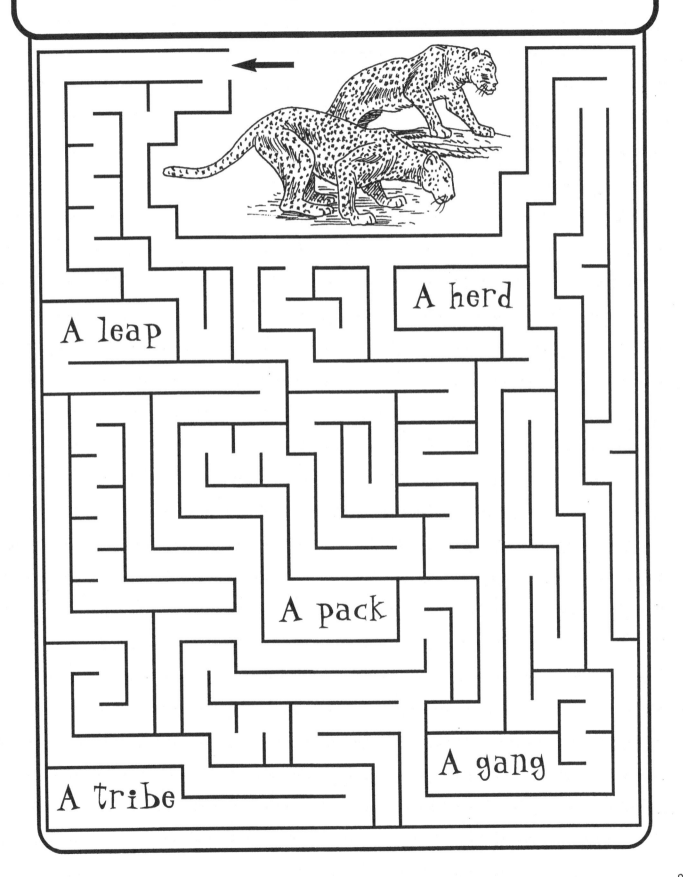

A leap

A herd

A pack

A tribe

A gang

What is the continent where the fewest dinosaur bones have been found?

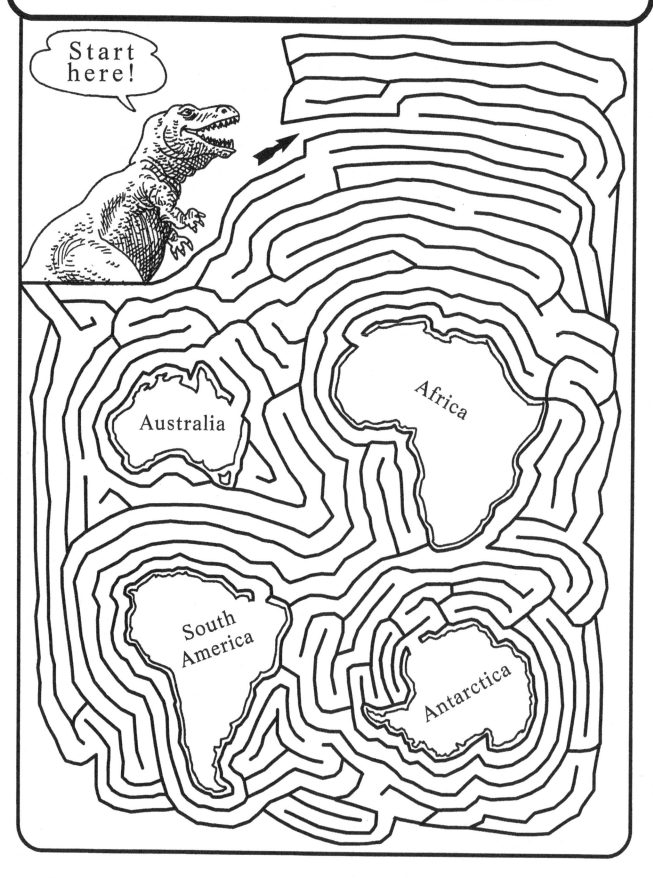

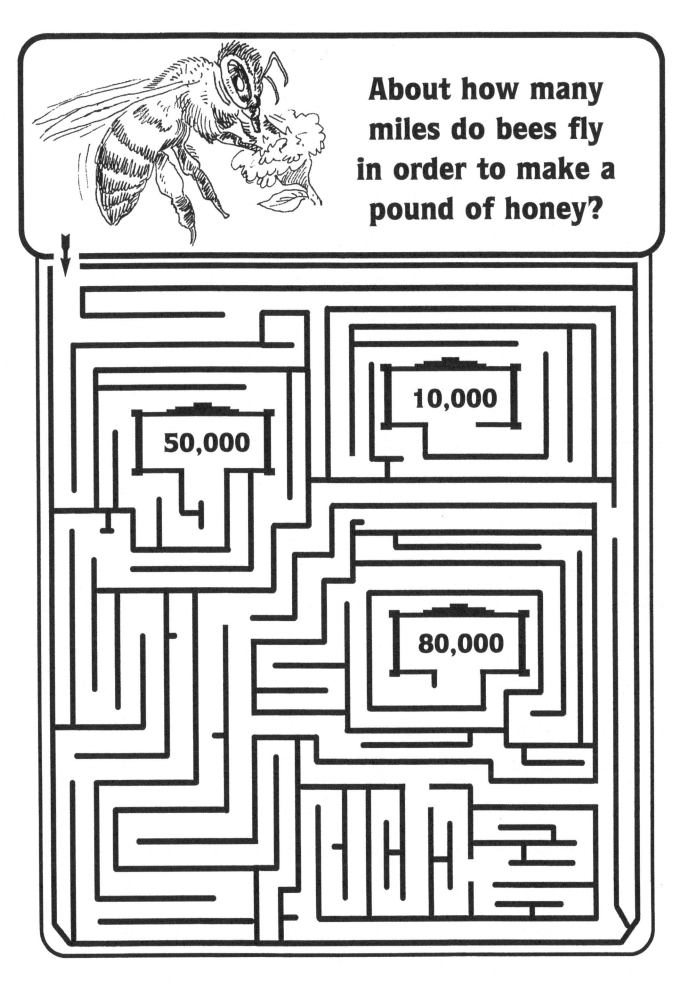

About how many miles do bees fly in order to make a pound of honey?

50,000

10,000

80,000

How many eggs does the average hen lay in a year?

19 dozen

Start

24 dozen

12 dozen

This animal can live longer than a camel can without water!

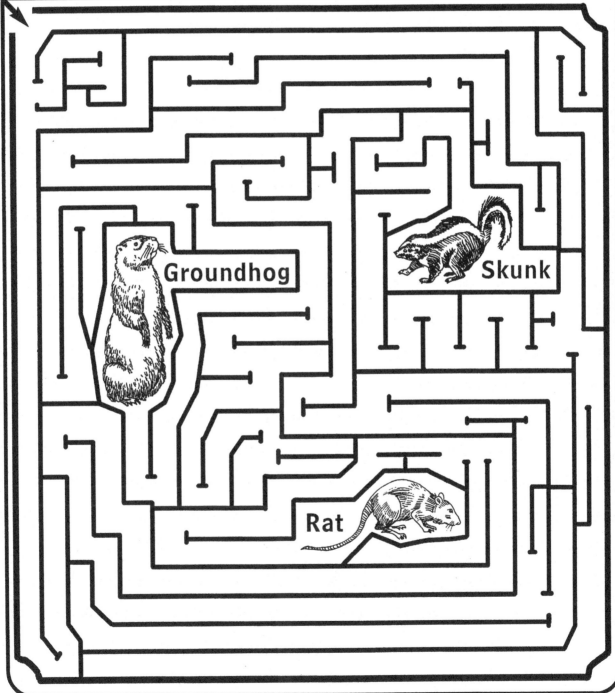

Groundhog

Skunk

Rat

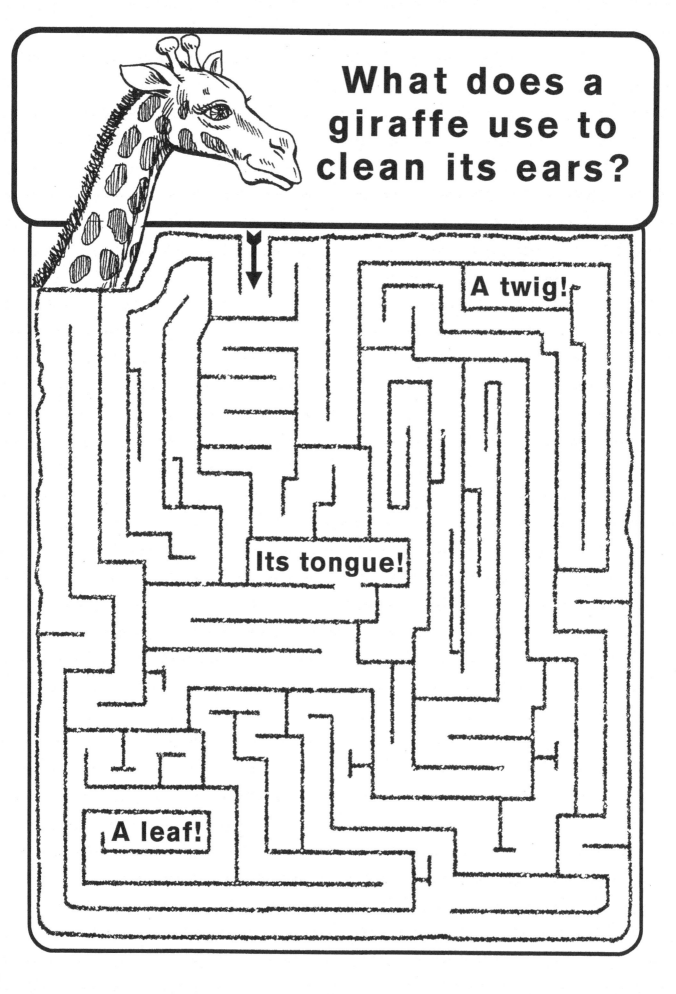

How many eyelids does a camel have on each eye?

What is the heaviest land animal?

What do an ostrich, an emu, a penguin, and a kiwi have in common?

All are nocturnal

All are black & white

None can fly

What is the largest and loudest animal on Earth? Its heart is the size of a small car and its call is louder than a jet plane!

North Pacific Giant Octopus

Great White Shark

Blue Whale

Which insect has the strongest legs? It can jump 500 times its own height!

Flea

Termite

START HERE

Praying Mantis

Grasshopper

Butterflies, moths, bees, and flies use this part of their body for tasting food.

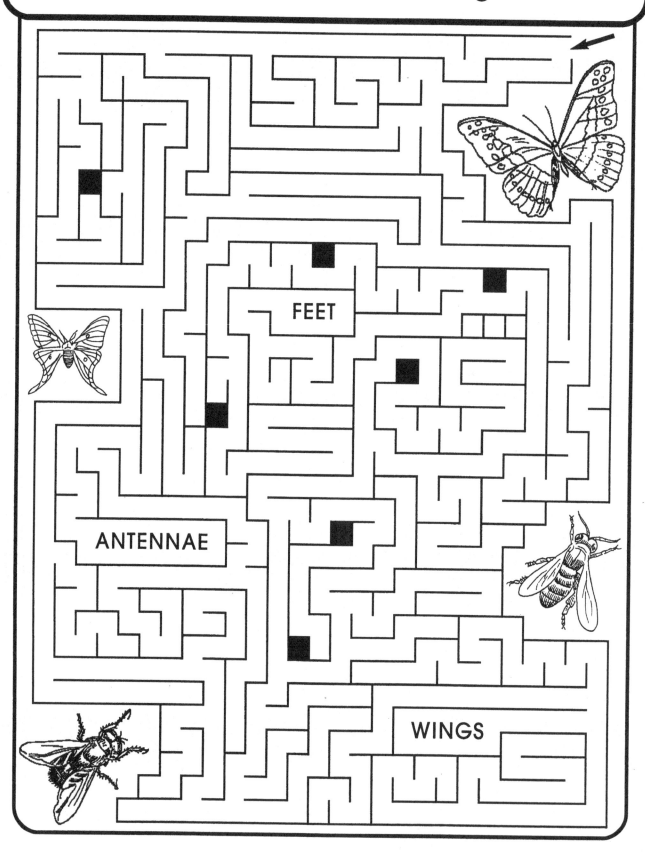

What is the greatest number of insects you might find in a square yard of soil?

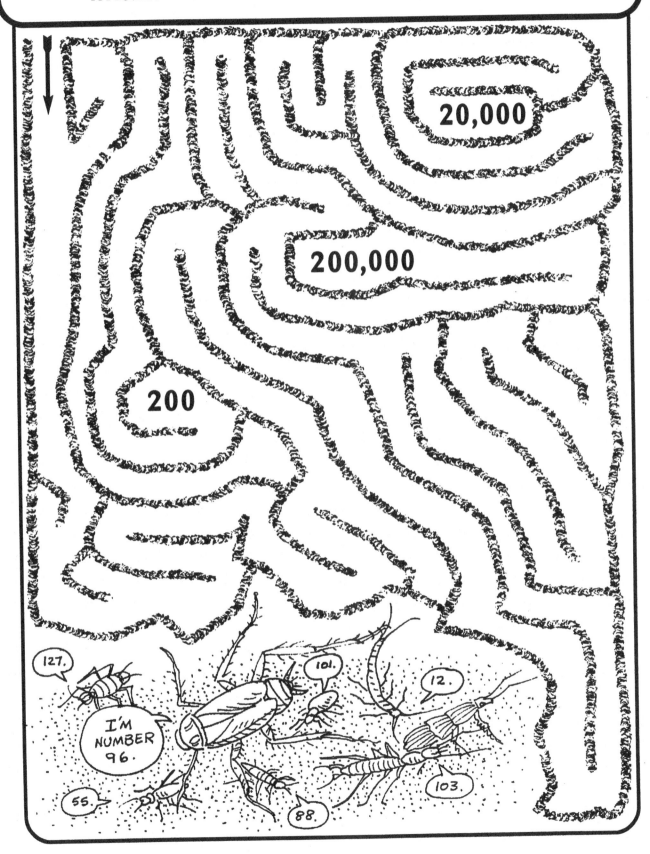

WHAT IS THE COLDEST AND WINDIEST PLACE ON EARTH?

NORTH POLE

ANTARCTICA

SIBERIA

ALASKA

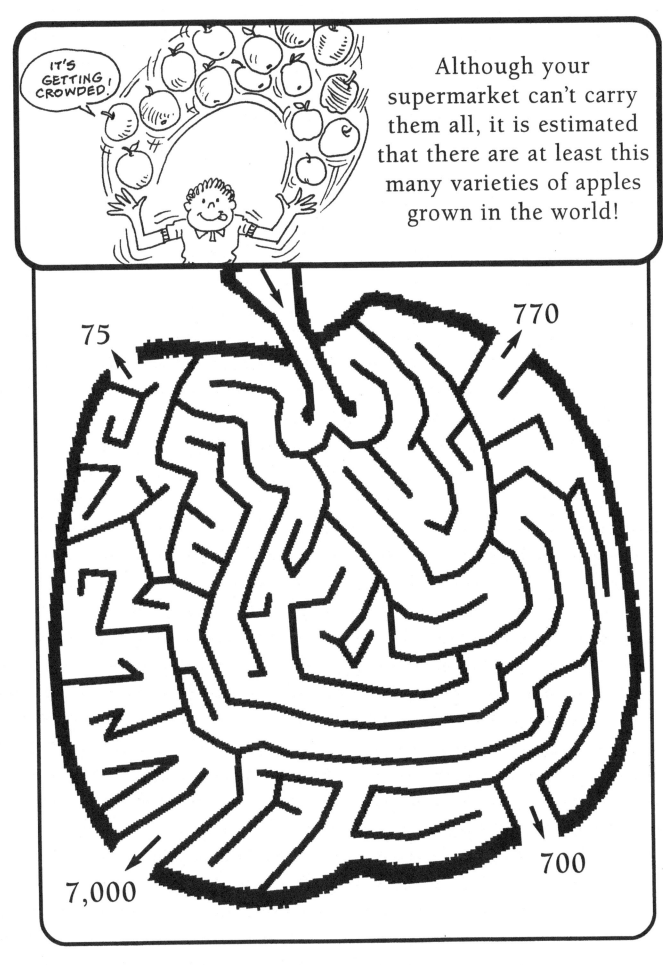

Lightning bolts hurtle toward Earth about 100 times every ...

Although no two snowflakes are exactly alike, they all share this number of sides or points.

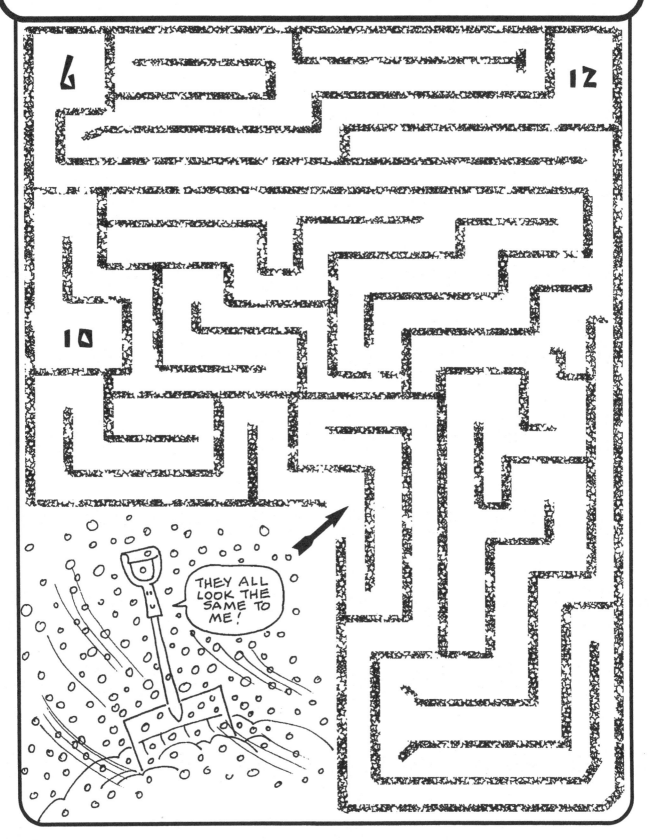

What are the tallest living things on Earth?

Giant Saguaro Cactus

Redwood Trees

Royal Palm Trees

Giraffes

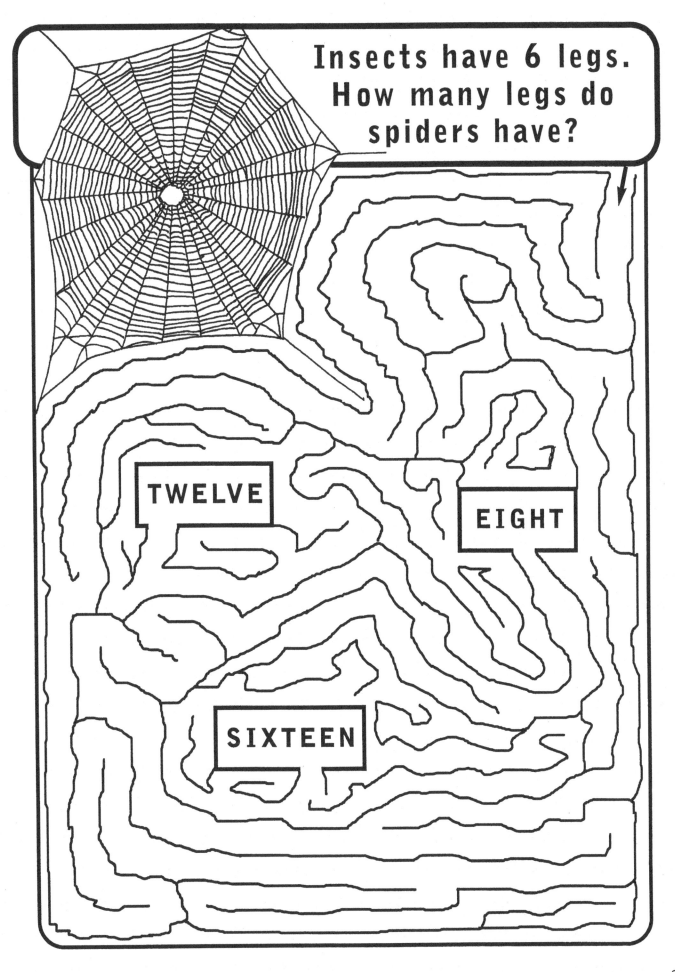

It takes both the sun and rain to make a rainbow. Into how many colors does the solar light—reflected in the raindrops—separate?

SEVEN COLORS

FIVE COLORS

EIGHT COLORS

What is the slowest-moving animal on Earth?

YUM!

How many taste buds are on the average human tongue?

10,000

4,000

1,000

20,000

It takes 43 muscles to frown. How many muscles do you use when you smile?

start here

Although high in calories, which fruit has more nutrition than any other?

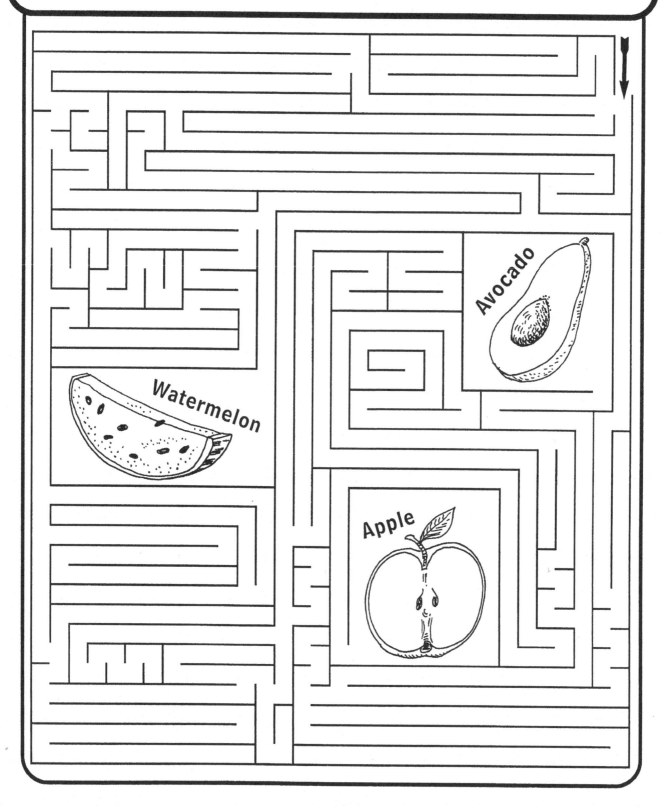

A single pair of these birds holds the record for the biggest nest ever built. Some of their nests weigh well over a thousand pounds!

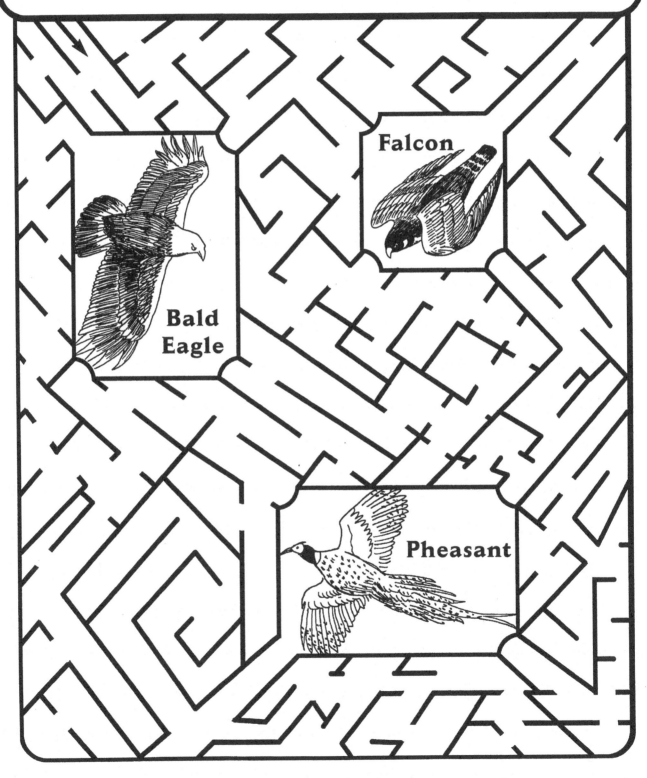

Falcon

Bald
Eagle

Pheasant

Which bird lays the biggest egg?

Moa

Dodo

Ostrich

What is the hardest natural substance on Earth?

Start here!

Silver

Diamonds

Gold

35

Which one of these mammals can't jump?

BEAVER

PIG

ELEPHANT

start here

How many muscles do cats have in each ear?

22

32

12

Which of these creatures sleeps with both eyes open?

SNAKES

BIRDS

GORILLAS

How many months does it take for your fingernail to grow from the base to the tip?

6

9

2

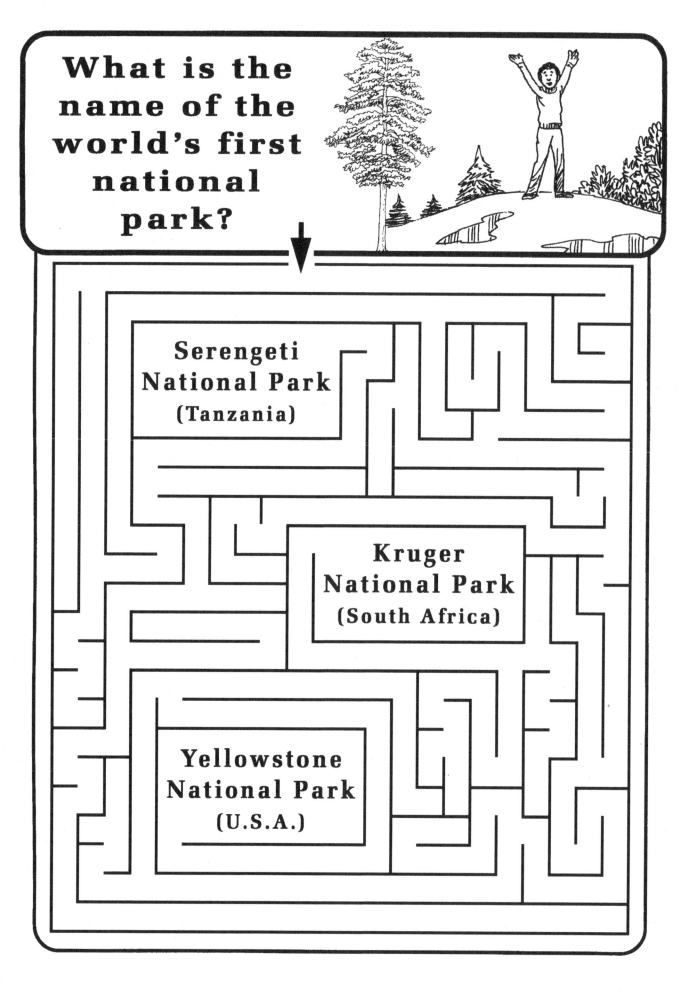

What is the name of the world's first national park?

Serengeti National Park (Tanzania)

Kruger National Park (South Africa)

Yellowstone National Park (U.S.A.)

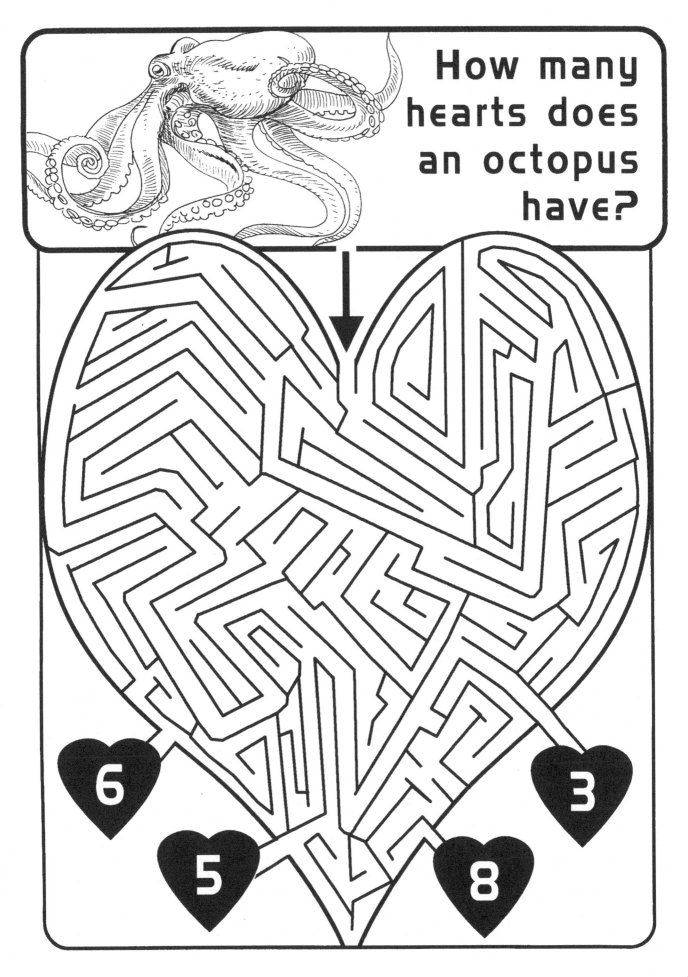

How many hearts does an octopus have?

6 5 8 3

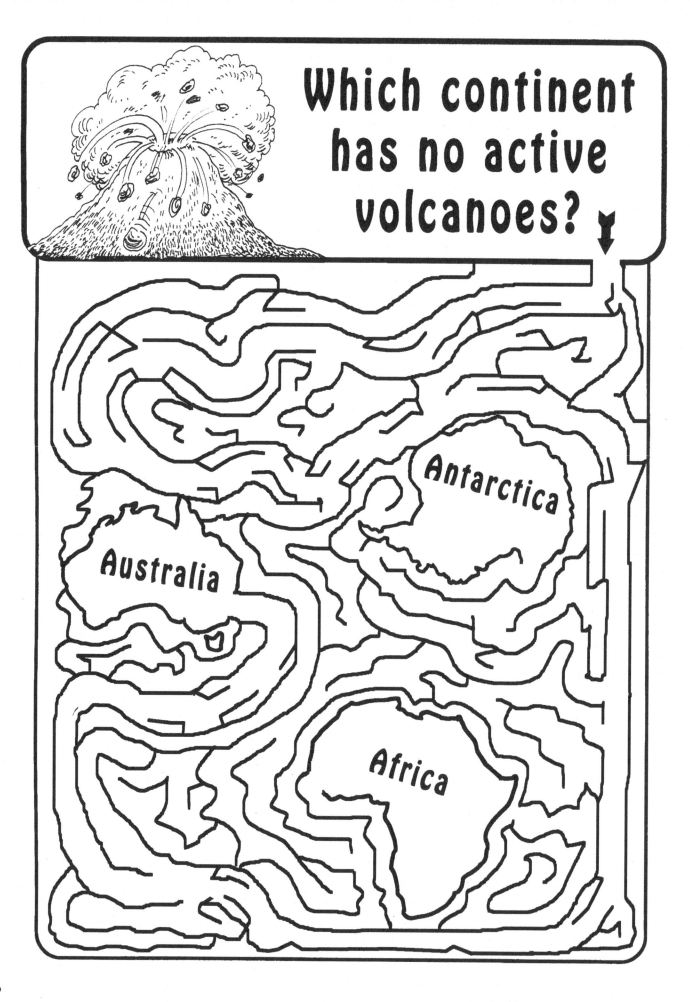

SOLUTIONS

The cheetah can reach a speed of 70 M.P.H., making it the fastest animal in the world. What is the second fastest animal, with a speed of up to 61 M.P.H.?

Page 1

What color are flamingoes when they are born? (It's not pink!)

RED WHITE GRAY BEIGE

Page 2

Which of these dogs is known as the "barkless dog"?

TERRIER KOMONDOR

BASENJI CORGI

Page 3

Americans eat more of these than any kind of fresh fruit, averaging over 25 pounds of them per person, per year!

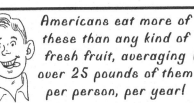

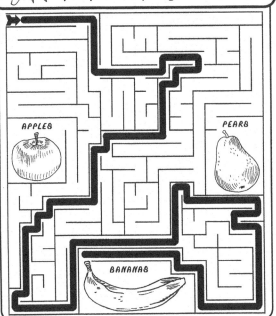

APPLES PEARS

BANANAS

Page 4

What family of animals does the koala belong to?

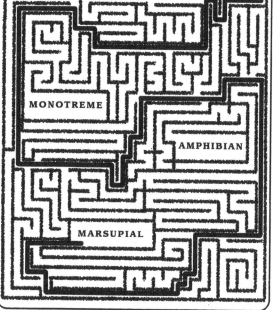

MONOTREME

AMPHIBIAN

MARSUPIAL

Page 5

A PEANUT IS NOT A NUT! WHAT IS IT?

A SEPAL

A GLUME

A LEGUME

Page 6

HOW MANY GALLONS OF WATER CAN A PELICAN'S POUCH HOLD?

3 GALLONS

6 GALLONS

4 GALLONS

Page 7

This is the largest of all rodents. A fully grown adult can weigh over 100 pounds!

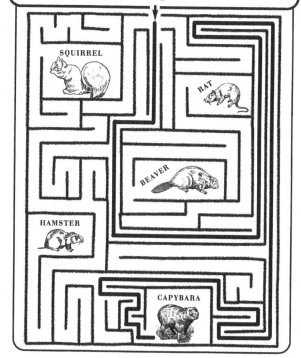

SQUIRREL

RAT

BEAVER

HAMSTER

CAPYBARA

Page 8

What is a group of leopards called?

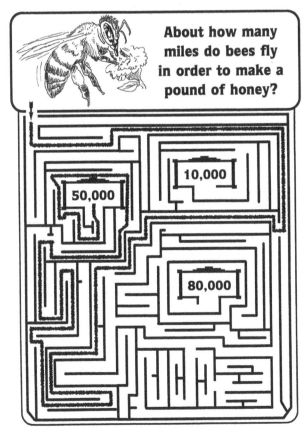

A leap

A herd

A pack

A tribe

A gang

Page 9

What is the continent where the fewest dinosaur bones have been found?

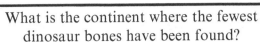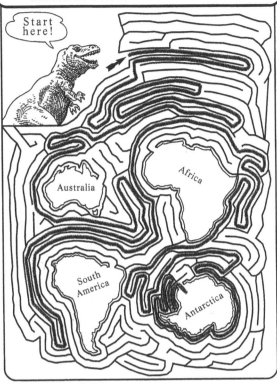

Start here!

Australia

Africa

South America

Antarctica

Page 10

About how many miles do bees fly in order to make a pound of honey?

10,000

50,000

80,000

Page 11

How many eggs does the average hen lay in a year?

19 dozen

Start

24 dozen

12 dozen

Page 12

This animal can live longer than a camel can without water!

Groundhog

Skunk

Rat

Page 13

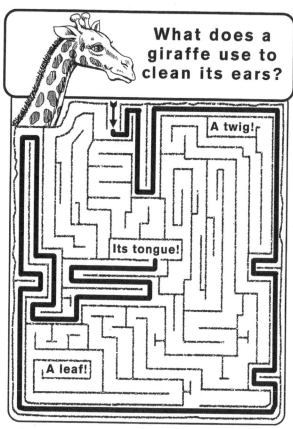

What does a giraffe use to clean its ears?

A twig!

Its tongue!

A leaf!

Page 14

How many eyelids does a camel have on each eye?

4

2

3

Page 15

What is the heaviest land animal?

KEEP JOGGING!

Giraffe

Elephant

HOW TO STAY ON A DIET!

Hippopotamus

I'M HUNGRY!

Rhinoceros

Page 16

52

What do an ostrich, an emu, a penguin, and a kiwi have in common?

All are nocturnal

All are black & white

None can fly

Page 17

What is the largest and loudest animal on Earth? Its heart is the size of a small car and its call is louder than a jet plane!

North Pacific Giant Octopus

Great White Shark

Blue Whale

Page 18

Which insect has the strongest legs? It can jump 500 times its own height!

Flea

Termite

START HERE

Praying Mantis

Grasshopper

Page 19

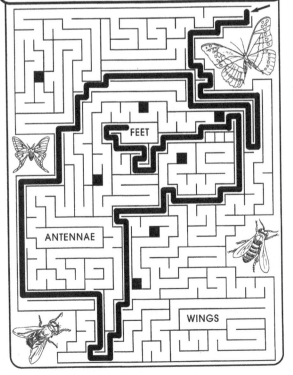

Butterflies, moths, bees, and flies use this part of their body for tasting food.

FEET

ANTENNAE

WINGS

Page 20

What is the greatest number of insects you might find in a square yard of soil?

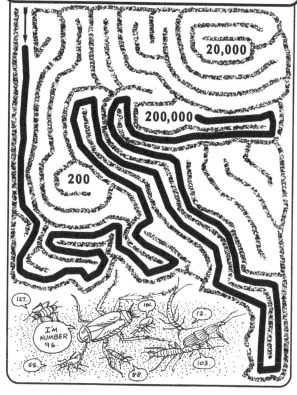

Page 21

WHAT IS THE COLDEST AND WINDIEST PLACE ON EARTH?

Page 22

Although your supermarket can't carry them all, it is estimated that there are at least this many varieties of apples grown in the world!

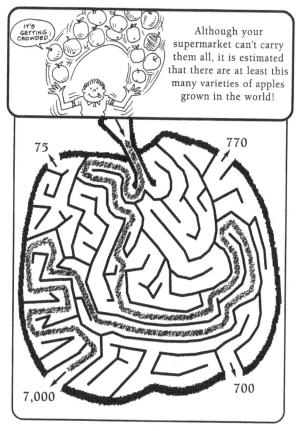

Page 23

Lightning bolts hurtle toward Earth about 100 times every ...

Page 24

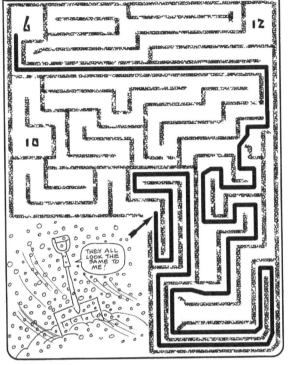

Page 25

What are the tallest living things on Earth?

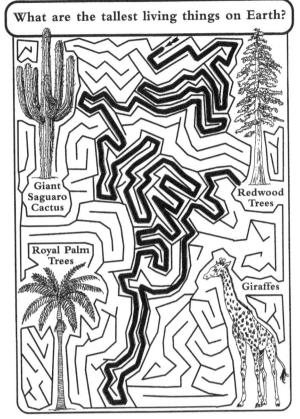

Page 26

Insects have 6 legs. How many legs do spiders have?

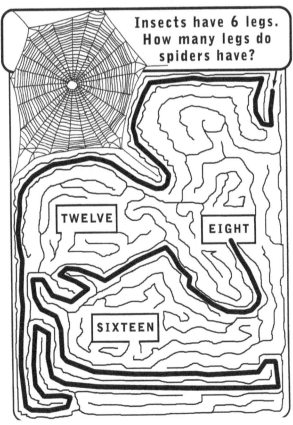

Page 27

It takes both the sun and rain to make a rainbow. Into how many colors does the solar light—reflected in the raindrops—separate?

Page 28

What is the slowest-moving animal on Earth?

Page 29

How many taste buds are on the average human tongue?

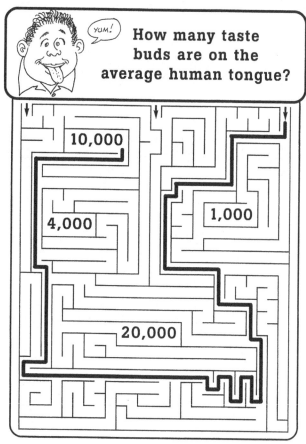

Page 30

It takes 43 muscles to frown. How many muscles do you use when you smile?

Page 31

Although high in calories, which fruit has more nutrition than any other?

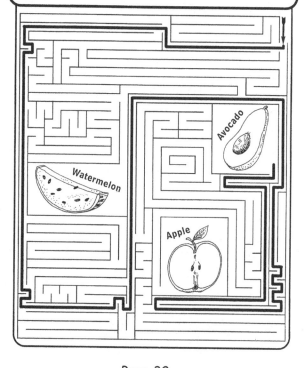

Page 32

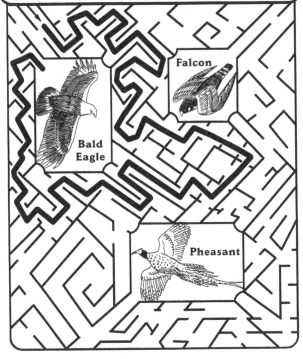

A single pair of these birds holds the record for the biggest nest ever built. Some of their nests weigh well over a thousand pounds!

Falcon

Bald Eagle

Pheasant

Page 33

Which bird lays the biggest egg?

Moa

Dodo

Ostrich

Page 34

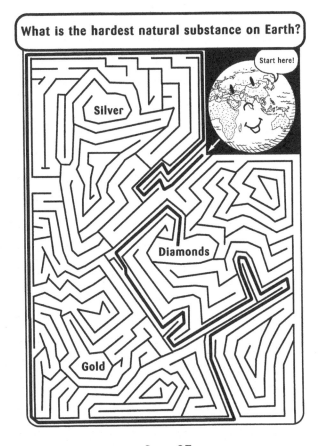

What is the hardest natural substance on Earth?

Start here!

Silver

Diamonds

Gold

Page 35

How many stars make up the Big Dipper?

6

5   7   9

Page 36

Page 37

How long can a blue whale go without eating?

Five Weeks

One Year

Six Months

Which one of these mammals can't jump?

PIG

BEAVER

ELEPHANT

start here

Page 38

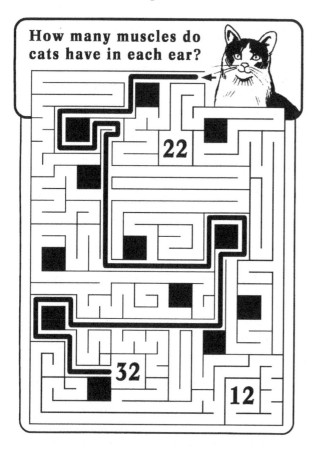

How many muscles do cats have in each ear?

22

32

12

Page 39

Which of these creatures sleeps with both eyes open?

SNAKES

BIRDS

GORILLAS

Page 40

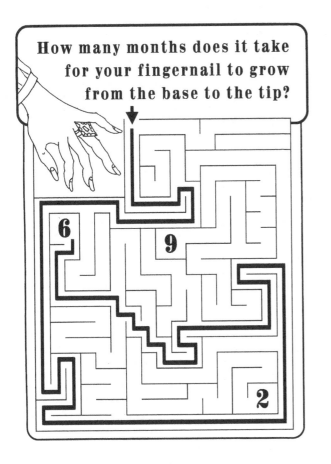

Page 41

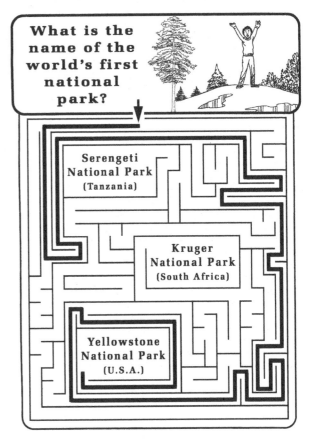

Page 42

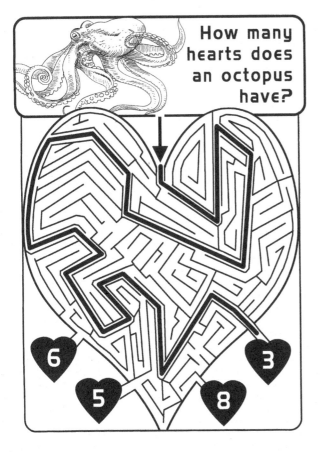

Page 43

Page 44

Page 45

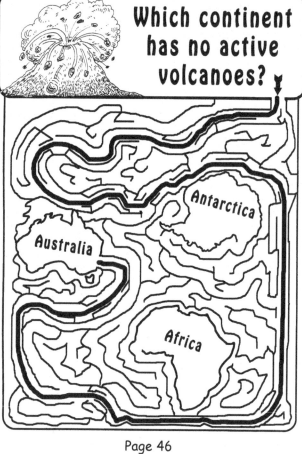

Page 46